What Narcissism Means to Me

Other Books by Tony Hoagland

Donkey Gospel

Sweet Ruin

WHAT
NARCISSISM
MEANS
TO ME

Tony Hoagland

Graywolf Press
Saint Paul, Minnesota

Publication of this volume is made possible in part by a grant provided by the Minnesota State Arts Board, through an appropriation by the Minnesota State Legislature; a grant from the Wells Fargo Foundation Minnesota; and a grant from the National Endowment for the Arts. Significant support has also been provided by the Bush Foundation; Target, Marshall Field's and Mervyn's with support from the Target Foundation; the McKnight Foundation; and other generous contributions from foundations, corporations, and individuals. To these organizations and individuals we offer our heartfelt thanks.

Published by GraywolfPress
2402 University Avenue, Suite 203
Saint Paul, Minnesota 55114
All rights reserved.

www.graywolfpress.org

Published in the United States of America

ISBN 978-1-55597-386-5

8 10 12 14 13 11 9 7

Library of Congress Control Number: 2003101172

Cover art: Pandit Seu (attributed), *A Dancer Performing with Two Musicians Who Play a Trumpet and a Drum* (detail), Guler, ca. 1730

Cover design: Jeanne Lee

Acknowledgments

Many thanks to the following journals, in which these poems first appeared:

88: "Argentina," "Poem in Which I Make the Mistake of Comparing
    Billie Holiday to a Cosmic Washerwoman"
Agni: "The Change"
American Poetry Review: "Catechism for November," "A Color of the Sky,"
    "America," "When Dean Young Talks about Wine," "Impossible
    Dream," "Grammar of Sparrows," "Migration," "The News,"
    "Still Life," "Man Carrying Sofa," "Two Trains," "The Time Wars,"
    "On the CD I Buy for My Brother"
Black Warrior Review: "How It Adds Up"
The Columbia Review: "Spring Lemonade"
Crazyhorse: "Appetite," "Phone Call"
Forklift: "Narcissus Lullaby"
Indiana Review: "Suicide Song"
Lyric: "Rap Music"
Massachusetts Review: "Commercial for a Summer Night"
Ploughshares: "Social Life," "Reasons to Survive November"
Slate: "Hate Hotel"
Threepenny Review: "Windchime"
TriQuarterly: "Disappointment"

I'm grateful to the John Simon Guggenheim Foundation for a fellowship
that supported the writing of these poems; also to the American Academy
of Arts and Letters. Thanks to George Washington University for their
Jenny McKean Moore Fellowship. Thanks to the friends who have sup-
ported me in the making of these poems, including, in particular, Dean
Young, Marie Howe, Neal Nixon, Richard McCann, Carl Dennis, Steve
Orlen, Peter Harris, Gibb Windahl, Terrance Hayes, Jane Shore, Jody Bolz,
Kathleen Lee, and JoAnn Beard. Very heartfelt thanks to Ken Hart and
Jason Shinder, for their meticulous, unflagging help with this manuscript.

"Still Life" is for Eleanor Wilner.

"Reasons to Survive November" is for JoAnn Beard.

"Windchime" is for B. S.

"Suicide Song" is for Gibb Windahl.

"Two Trains" is for Kevin McIlvoy.

"Commercial for a Summer Night" is for Toni Nelson and Robert Boswell.

"The Time Wars" is for Richard McCann.

Contents

for Kathleen Lee

What Narcissism Means to Me

Although Rama was Vishnu,
his human incarnation
made him unaware of his identity
at the moment.

The Ramayana,
trans. R. K. Narayan

Ugh! the stupidity of the beloved!

Grace Paley, "Love"

I. America

Commercial for a Summer Night

That one night in the middle of the summer
when people move their chairs outside
and put their TVs on the porch
so the dark is full of murmuring blue lights.

We were drinking beer with the sound off,
watching the figures on the screen—
the bony blondes, the lean-jawed guys
who decorate the perfume and the cars—

the pretty ones
the merchandise is wearing this year.

Alex said, *I wish they made a shooting gallery*
            using people like that.

Greg said, *That woman has a Ph.D. in Face.*
Then we saw a preview for a movie

about a movie star who is
            having a movie made about her,
and Boz said, *This country is getting stupider every year.*

Then Greg said that things were better in the sixties
and Rus said that Harold Bloom said
that Nietzsche said Nostalgia
is the blank check issued to a weak mind,

and Greg said,
        They didn't have checks back then, stupid,
and Susan said It's too bad you guys can't get
Spellcheck for your brains.

Then Greg left and Margaret arrived
and a breeze carried honeysuckle fumes across the yard,
and Alex finished his quart of beer
and Boz leaned back in his chair

and the beautiful people on the TV screen
moved back and forth and back,
looking very much now like shooting-gallery ducks—

and we sat in quiet pleasure on the shore of night,
as a tide came in and turned and carried us,
folding chairs and all,

far out from the coastline of America

in a perfect commercial for our lives.

America

Then one of the students with blue hair and a tongue stud
Says that America is for him a maximum-security prison

Whose walls are made of RadioShacks and Burger Kings, and MTV episodes
Where you can't tell the show from the commercials,

And as I consider how to express how full of shit I think he is,
He says that even when he's driving to the mall in his Isuzu

Trooper with a gang of his friends, letting rap music pour over them
Like a boiling Jacuzzi full of ballpeen hammers, even then he feels

Buried alive, captured and suffocated in the folds
Of the thick satin quilt of America

And I wonder if this is a legitimate category of pain,
or whether he is just spin doctoring a better grade,

And then I remember that when I stabbed my father in the dream last night,
It was not blood but money

That gushed out of him, bright green hundred-dollar bills
Spilling from his wounds, and—this is the weird part—,

He gasped, "Thank god—those Ben Franklins were
Clogging up my heart—

And so I perish happily,
Freed from that which kept me from my liberty"—

Which is when I knew it was a dream, since my dad
Would never speak in rhymed couplets,

And I look at the student with his acne and cell phone and phony ghetto
    clothes
And I think, "I am asleep in America too,

And I don't know how to wake myself either,"
And I remember what Marx said near the end of his life:

"I was listening to the cries of the past,
When I should have been listening to the cries of the future."

But how could he have imagined 100 channels of 24-hour cable
Or what kind of nightmare it might be

When each day you watch rivers of bright merchandise run past you
And you are floating in your pleasure boat upon this river

Even while others are drowning underneath you
And you see their faces twisting in the surface of the waters

And yet it seems to be your own hand
Which turns the volume higher?

Argentina

What I notice today is the aroma of my chiropractor's breath
as he moves in over my supineness, asking me where I bought those shoes
at the same instant that he
                              wrenches my head abruptly sidewise
to crack my neck with a noise like popping bubblewrap.

It's January, no, it's February, it's Pittsburgh
and I've been so twisted by craving and loneliness and rage,
I feel like curling up on the floor of my room and crying,
"You never loved me anyway, not ever!"
though I'm not sure who I would be talking to.

Kath says February is always like eating a raw egg;
Peter says it's like wearing a bandage on your head;
Mary says it's like a pack of wild dogs who have gotten into medical waste,
        and smiles because she clearly is the winner.

And in Argentina, after the elections,
we hear the old president won't leave office—
literally, they say—they can't get him out of the office!
He's in there with his little private army, eating caviar,
squandering state money on call girls and porno movies—
and if you've done any therapy at all, I think you'll see the analogy.

How did I come to believe in a government called Tony Hoagland?
with an economy based on flattery and self-protection?
and a sewage system of selective forgetting?
and an extensive history of broken promises?

What did I get in exchange for my little bargain? What did I lose?
Where are my natural resources, my principal imports,
and why is my landscape so full of stony ridges and granite outcroppings?

Having said that much,
having paid a stranger to touch and straighten me,
I walk out the door to my old car in the parking lot
—which, after the slight adjustment of a spring shower,
                            looks almost new again.

The Change

The season turned like the page of a glossy fashion magazine.
In the park the daffodils came up
and in the parking lot, the new car models were on parade.

Sometimes I think that nothing really changes—

The young girls show the latest crop of tummies,
        and the new president proves that he's a dummy.

But remember the tennis match we watched that year?
Right before our eyes

some tough little European blonde
pitted against that big black girl from Alabama,
cornrowed hair and Zulu bangles on her arms,
some outrageous name like Vondella Aphrodite—

We were just walking past the lounge
        and got sucked in by the screen above the bar,
and pretty soon
we started to care about who won,

putting ourselves into each whacked return
as the volleys went back and forth and back
like some contest between
the old world and the new,

and you loved her complicated hair
and her to-hell-with-everybody stare,
and I,
        I couldn't help wanting
the white girl to come out on top,

because she was one of my kind, my tribe,
with her pale eyes and thin lips

and because the black girl was so big
and so black,
                    so unintimidated,

hitting the ball like she was driving the Emancipation Proclamation
down Abraham Lincoln's throat,
like she wasn't asking anyone's permission.

There are moments when history
passes you so close
                    you can smell its breath,
you can reach your hand out
                                        and touch it on its flank,

and I don't watch all that much *Masterpiece Theatre,*
but I could feel the end of an era there

in front of those bleachers full of people
in their Sunday tennis-watching clothes

as that black girl wore down her opponent
then kicked her ass good
then thumped her once more for good measure

and stood up on the red clay court
holding her racket over her head like a guitar.

And the little pink judge
                    had to climb up on a box
to put the ribbon on her neck,

still managing to smile into the camera flash,
even though everything was changing

and in fact, everything had already changed—

Poof, remember? It was the twentieth century almost gone,
we were there,

and when we went to put it back where it belonged,
it was past us
and we were changed.

When Dean Young Talks about Wine

The worm thrashes when it enters the tequila.
The grape cries out in the wine vat crusher.

But when Dean Young talks about wine, his voice is strangely calm.
Yet it seems that wine is rarely mentioned.

He says, Great first chapter but no plot.
He says, Long runway, short flight.
He says, This one never had a secret.
He says, You can't wear stripes with that.

He squints as if recalling his childhood in France.
He purses his lips and shakes his head at the glass.

Eighty-four was a naughty year, he says,
and for a second I worry that California has turned him
into a sushi-eater in a cravat.

Then he says,
                    This one makes clear the difference
between a thoughtless remark
and an unwarranted intrusion.

Then he says, In this one the pacific last light of afternoon
stains the wings of the seagull pink
                    at the very edge of the postcard.

But where is the Cabernet of rent checks and asthma medication?
Where is the Burgundy of orthopedic shoes?
Where is the Chablis of skinned knees and jelly sandwiches?
with the aftertaste of cruel Little League coaches?
and the undertone of rusty stationwagon?

His mouth is purple as if from his own ventricle
he had drunk.
He sways like a fishing rod.

When a beast is hurt it roars in incomprehension.
When a bird is hurt it huddles in its nest.

But when a man is hurt,
                he makes himself an expert.
Then he stands there with a glass in his hand
staring into nothing
                as if he was forming an opinion.

What Narcissism Means to Me

There's Socialism and Communism and Capitalism,
said Neal,
and there's Feminism and Hedonism,
          and there's Catholicism and Bipedalism and Consumerism,

but I think Narcissism is the system
that means the most to me;

and Sylvia said that in Neal's case
narcissism represented a heroic achievement in positive thinking.

And Ann,
who calls everybody Sweetie pie
          whether she cares for them or not,

Ann lit a cigarette and said, Only miserable people will tell you
          that love has to be deserved,

and when I heard that, a distant chime went off for me,

remembering a time when I believed
          that I could simply live without it.

Neal had grilled the corn and sliced the onions
               into thick white disks,
               and piled the wet green pickles
                    up in stacks like coins
          and his chef's cap was leaning sideways like a mushroom cloud.

Then Ethan said that in his opinion,
if you're going to mess around with self-love
          you shouldn't just rush into a relationship,

and Sylvia was weeping softly now, looking down
        into her wine cooler and potato chips,

and then the hamburgers were done, just as
the sunset in the background started
                cutting through the charcoal clouds

exposing their insides—black,
streaked dark red,
            like a slab of scorched, rare steak,

delicious but unhealthy,
or, depending on your perspective,
                unhealthy but delicious,

—the way that, deep inside the misery
        of daily life,
                love lies bleeding.

Impossible Dream

In Delaware a congressman
          accused of sexual misconduct
says clearly at the press conference,
   speaking
            right into the microphone,
that he would like very much
                to do it again.

It was on the radio
          and Carla laughed
as she painted, *Die, You Pig*
           in red nail polish
on the back of a turtle
she plans to turn loose tomorrow
           in Jerry's backyard.

We lived near the high school that year
and in the afternoons, in autumn,
you could hear the marching-band rehearsals
from the stadium:
           off-key trumpets carried by the wind,
drums and weirdly smeared trombones:

a ragged "Louie Louie"
    or sometimes, "The Impossible Dream."

I was reading a book about pleasure,
how you have to glide through it
           without clinging,
like an arrow
passing through a target,
          coming out the other side and going on.

Sitting at the picnic table
carved with the initials of the previous tenants;
                    thin October sunlight
blessing the pale grass—
you would have said we had it all—

But the turtle in Carla's hand
churned its odd, stiff legs like oars,
as if it wasn't made for holding still,

and the high-school band played
                    worse than ever for a moment
—as if getting the song right
                    was the impossible dream.

Parade

Peter says if you're going to talk about suffering
you have to mention pleasure too.

Like the way, on the day of the parade, on Forbes Avenue,
one hundred parking tickets flutter
under the windshield wipers of one hundred parked cars.

The accordion band will be along soon,
and the famous Flying Pittsburgettes,
and it's summer and the sun is shining on the inevitable flags—

Something weird to admire this week on TV:
the handsome face of the white supremacist on trial.
How he looks right back at the lawyers, day after day
—never objecting, never making an apology.

I look at his calm, untroubled face
and think, *That motherfucker is going to die white and right,*
            disappointing everyone like me
who thinks that punishment should be a kind of education.

My attitude is like what God says in the Bible:
            Love your brother, or be destroyed.
Then Moses or somebody says back to God,
         If I love you,
                  will you destroy my enemies?
and God says—this is in translation—, *No Problemo.*

Here, everyone is talking about the price of freedom,
and about how we as a people are united in our down payment,
about how we will fight to the very bottom of our bank account.

And the sky is so blue it looks like it may last forever
and the skinny tuba player goes *oompahpah,*
and everybody cheers.

In the big store window of the travel agency downtown,
a ten-foot sign says, WE WILL NEVER FORGET.

The letters have been cut with scissors out of blue construction paper
and pasted carefully to the sign by someone's hand.

What I want to know is, who will issue the ticket
                    for improper use of the collective pronoun?
What I want to know is, who will find and punish the maker
                    of these impossible promises?

Still Life

The French have it wrong, said Larry;
the self isn't a historical fiction or a cultural construct
                              or a linguistic hallucination;
the self is a creature
and it lives in a burrow
          under the hillside of history

a modest animal   like a badger or a vole
rarely seen   resourceful
neither beautiful nor ugly but merely alive—

And he smiled briefly, like a sad child
who feels secretly a little proud for being sad,

—and, making sure
there was a wall behind him,

he tipped back, carefully, in his chair.

II. Social Life

Social Life

After the first party peters out,
like the gradual slowdown of a merry-go-round,
 another party begins

and the survivors of the first party
climb onto the second one
 and start it up again.

Behind me now my friend Richard
is getting a fresh drink; Ann, in her black dress,
is fanning her breasts; Cynthia is prancing
from group to group,
 making kissy-face—

It is not given to me to understand
the social pleasures of my species, but I think
what they get from these affairs
is what bees get from flowers—a nudging of the stamen,

a sprinkle of pollen
about the head and shoulders—

whereas I prefer the feeling of going away, going away,
stretching out my distance from the voices and the lights
until the tether breaks and I

am in the wild sweet dark
where the sea breeze sizzles in the hedgetop,

and the big weed heads, whose names I never learned,
lift and nod upon their stalks.

What I like about the trees is how
they do not talk about the failure of their parents
and what I like about the grasses is that
they are not grasses in recovery

and what I like about the flowers is
that they are not flowers in need of
empowerment or validation. They sway

upon their thorny stems
as if whatever was about to happen next tonight
was sure to be completely interesting—

the moon rising like an ivory tusk,
a few sextillion molecules of skunk
strolling through the air
to mingle with the aura of a honeysuckle bush,

and when they bump together in my nose,
I want to raise my head and sing,
I'm a child in paradise again
when you touch me like that, baby,

but instead, I stand still and listen
to the breeze streaming through the upper story of a tree
and the hum of insects in the field,
letting everything else have a word,

and then another word—
because silence is always good manners
and often a clever thing to say
when you are at a party.

A Color of the Sky

Windy today and I feel less than brilliant,
driving over the hills from work.
There are the dark parts on the road
                when you pass through clumps of wood
and the bright spots where you have a view of the ocean,
but that doesn't make the road an allegory.

I should call Marie and apologize
for being so boring at dinner last night,
but can I really promise not to be that way again?
And anyway, I'd rather watch the trees, tossing
in what certainly looks like sexual arousal.

Otherwise it's spring, and everything looks frail;
the sky is baby blue, and the just-unfurling leaves
are full of infant chlorophyll,
the very tint of inexperience.

Last summer's song is making a comeback on the radio,
and on the highway overpass,
the only metaphysical vandal in America has written
MEMORY LOVES TIME
in big black spraypaint letters,

which makes us wonder if Time loves Memory back.

Last night I dreamed of X again.
She's like a stain on my subconscious sheets.
Years ago she penetrated me
but though I scrubbed and scrubbed and scrubbed,
I never got her out,
but now I'm glad.

What I thought was an end turned out to be a middle.
What I thought was a brick wall turned out to be a tunnel.
What I thought was an injustice
turned out to be a color of the sky.

Outside the youth center, between the liquor store
and the police station,
a little dogwood tree is losing its mind;

overflowing with blossomfoam,
like a sudsy mug of beer;
like a bride ripping off her clothes,

dropping snow white petals to the ground in clouds,

so Nature's wastefulness seems quietly obscene.
It's been doing that all week:
making beauty,
and throwing it away,
and making more.

Dear John

I never would have told John that faggot joke
        if I had known that he was gay;
I really shot myself in the foot with that Neanderthal effort
to make a witty first impression.

I thought he was just a skinny guy from New York City
with clean hands and allergies, come to a Vermont
he knew mainly from the pictures on the side
        of a gallon can of Log Cabin maple syrup.

I could tell he was nervous about how real the maples really were,
and the guys in their flannel shirts and dirty hiking boots,
so I made my tasteless remark to put him at his ease.
That was before male idiocy had been

officially recognized as a chemical imbalance,
but he forgave me and let me be his friend,
and if I can say so without sounding patriotic about myself,
there's something democratic

about being the occasional asshole—
you make a mistake, you apologize
        and everyone else breathes easier—
John helped me through the whole lesbian thing

when Margie decided to take her feminism
in a recreational direction, and I got him a recording
of simulated gunfire and police sirens
to help him sleep through the towering
        old-growth silence of the Vermont night.

He still calls sometimes, when his phone and memory
are working at the same time, and

I don't know what he does for sex or money,
but it's taken me a decade to recognize that I love John,

—not for his cuteness (he is)
or for his endearing manner of being always on the brink
        of falling apart,
but precisely because he doesn't ever threaten to love me back.

On someone like that you can lavish your affection
in perfect safety—
that's nothing to be proud of, I suppose—
and yet, obscurely, I am.

Leaving Yourself Behind

Carrie says it's more rude to stare at a blind man on the street
than to make a fat-person joke about someone on TV.

Her hyperborean ethical principles would be funny
                                  if she didn't take them seriously,
blinking back tears of compassion, unable to finish her Jell-O in the
    cafeteria.

Then she gets up to go, leaving a mess on the tray
                                 for the Mexican busboy to clear.
Vain and self-destructive, brilliant, well-behaved
                                 when she isn't being hysterical,

terrible lines are forming a conspiracy in her face
as in that '60s song about a broken-hearted teenager,
                                 called "The Tracks of My Tears."

If gratuitous suffering paid even minimum wage,
and Carrie kept track of her hours,
she could be behind the wheel of a late-model car by now,

driving through life with low mileage and a smooth suspension.
Instead, she's walking by the side of the road,

getting more and more mud on her boots,
just like the rest of us.

Patience

"Success is the worst possible thing that could happen
                          to a man like you," she said,
"because the shiny shoes, and flattery
                          and the self-
lubricating slime of affluence would mean
you'd never have to face your failure as a human being."

There was a rude remark I could have made back to her right then
and I watched it go by like a bright blue sailboat on a long gray river
                                        of silence,
watching it until it disappeared around the bend

while I smiled and listened to her talk,
thinking it was good to let myself be stabbed by her little spears,
because I wanted to see what I was made of

besides fear and the desire to be liked
by every person on the goddamn face of the earth—

To tell the truth, I felt a certain satisfaction in taking it,

letting her believe that I was just a little bird
opening my mouth and swallowing
                          the medicine she wanted to administer

—a mixture of good advice combined with slow-acting poison.

Is it strange to say that there was something beautiful
in the sight of her running wild, cut loose in an
                          epileptic fit of telling the truth?

And anyway, she was right about me,
that I am prone to certain misperceptions,

that I should never get so big or fat that I
can't look down and see my own naked dirty feet,

which is why I kept smiling and smiling as she talked—.

It was a beautiful day. I felt like crying.

I knew that if I could succeed at being demolished,
I could succeed at anything.

Appetite

There are three of us in the restaurant
where I have dinner with my friend
—me, him, and one of those diseases
                    known by its initials.

There's a recently amputated rose
in a jar at table center
and in the kitchen, just this minute,
a lobster with my name on it
is being carried toward a kettle,
which doesn't bother me.

What bothers me
is how I imagine I can see
the virus looking out
from his dullish-bright dark eyes,
and the peculiar gusto
with which he eats and drinks,

taking two of everything,
touching all his food before he swallows it—
the bread, the crumpled dark green
money of the lettuce
entering his mouth, which keeps
on talking while he chews,

telling me how good life is now that he is
living on the edge,
now that he is tasting every bite—

until a weird contagious glow
creeps into our corner of the room,
and in that X-ray light

I can see the blackness hidden
in the tissues of the rose,
the sooty funeral procession just setting out
from the frail, veined
                    edges of each petal,

and the pimples on the busboy's chin
ripen toward their bursting
                    moment of perfection.

How horrible it is to be alive,
to wake one day to feel the earth
begin to seethe and writhe beneath your feet—

the wilderness outside you pressing to get in,
the wilderness inside you trying to get out,
the tangled, penetrating vines,
                    the compost stink.

And in the jungle of my brain
I can hear the thoughts now
          chewing on the underside
of other thoughts,

and under them, the humming, shifting feelings
which feed on anything,
                    and under them
the ink of anti-thought, liquidly unlinking
the little chains—
and then a clinking sound *tink tink*
from far away

as my friend
strikes his fork against his water glass
to bring me back   *tink tink*
from wherever I am gone.

His plate is clean, his teeth are white,
his glass is raised. I understand
he wants to make a toast:
to Dream
and Appetite
and Night.

Reasons to Survive November

November like a train wreck—
as if a locomotive made of cold
had hurtled out of Canada
and crashed into a million trees,
flaming the leaves, setting the woods on fire.

The sky is a thick, cold gauze—
but there's a soup special at the Waffle House downtown,
and the Jack Parsons show is up at the museum,
full of luminous red barns.

—Or maybe I'll visit beautiful Donna,
the kickboxing queen from Santa Fe,
and roll around in her foldout bed.

I know there are some people out there
who think I am supposed to end up
                    in a room by myself

with a gun and a bottle full of hate,
a locked door and my slack mouth open
            like a disconnected phone.

But I hate those people back
from the core of my donkey soul
and the hatred makes me strong
and my survival is their failure,

and my happiness would kill them
so I shove joy like a knife
into my own heart over and over

and I force myself toward pleasure,
and I love this November life
where I run like a train
deeper and deeper
into the land of my enemies.

Wasteful Gesture Only Not

Ruth visits her mother's grave in the California hills.
She knows her mother isn't there but the rectangle of grass
marks off the place where the memories are kept,

like a library book named *Dorothy*.
Some of the chapters might be: *Dorothy:*
Better Bird-Watcher Than Cook;

Dorothy, Wife and Atheist;
Passionate Recycler Dorothy, Here Lies But Not.
In the summer hills, where the tall tough grass

reminds you of persistence
and the endless wind
reminds you of indifference,

Ruth brings batches of white roses,
extravagant gesture not entirely wasteful
because as soon as she is gone she knows
the deer come out of the woods to eat them.

What was made for the eye
goes into the mouth,
thinks Ruth to herself as she drives away,
and in bed when she tries to remember her mother,

she drifts instead to the roses,
and when she thinks about the roses she
sees instead the deer chewing them—

the pale petals of the roses in the dark
warm bellies of the sleeping deer—
that's what going to sleep is like.

Phone Call

Maybe I overdid it
when I called my father an enemy of humanity.
That might have been a little strongly put,
a slight overexaggeration,

an immoderate description of the person
who at that moment, two thousand miles away,
holding the telephone receiver six inches from his ear,
must have regretted paying for my therapy.

What I meant was that my father
was an enemy of *my* humanity
and what I meant behind that
was that my father was split
into two people, one of them

living deep inside of me
like a bad king or an incurable disease—
blighting my crops,
striking down my herds,
poisoning my wells—the other
standing in another time zone,
in a kitchen in Wyoming,
with bad knees and white hair sprouting from his ears.

I don't want to scream forever,
I don't want to live without proportion
like some kind of infection from the past,

so I have to remember the second father,
the one whose TV dinner is getting cold
while he holds the phone in his left hand
and stares blankly out the window

where just now the sun is going down
and the last fingertips of sunlight
are withdrawing from the hills
they once touched like a child.

Migration

This year Marie drives back and forth
from the hospital room of her dying friend
to the office of the adoption agency.

I bet sometimes she doesn't know
what threshold she is waiting at—

the hand of her sick friend, hot with fever;
the theoretical baby just a lot of paperwork so far.

But next year she might be standing by a grave,
wearing black with a splash of
                              banana vomit on it,

the little girl just starting to say *Sesame Street*
and *Cappuccino latte grande Mommy.*
The future ours for a while to hold, with its heaviness—

and hope moving from one location to another
like the holy ghost that it is.

III. Blues

On the CD I Buy for My Brother

A forlorn guy with a guitar
                issues bulletins from the coast of Melancholia,
plaintive dirges in which the macho and romantic
                      run together like two rivers
joined into a watershed area that could be called
                        Big Mississippi Pity Party,

and the singer is a loner with a boner
        and he's a Gomer and a moaner and a longtime roamer
and the moon in his rearview reminds him of a redhead
        in Natchez with a little anorexia problem
who danced the hoochie coochie clad in just a green bandana.

He says, *Love don't last but I recall her haid on the pillow*
                shorely was a purty sight;
he says, *Daylight's just a torn-open letter saying Larry I'm sorry.*

I mean this guy is always rowing upstream on the Bad Luck River
        with a rusty hubcap for a paddle

or looking downward from the precipice of I'm No Good
at the base of which an ocean of whiskey and beer
        has been performing erosion for years,

so it's possible that I am doing my brother no favor
by appealing to certain tendencies already in his disposition,

but then, why should I try to improve him on his birthday?
when at this stage of our lives what we are and what we aren't
        is so very apparent

and the grown-ups we once needed to please are endlessly silent

and the nights are long and hollow like the inside of a tunnel
and the train rushing through that tunnel is moving faster and faster
      and you know the cargo in those boxcars is some serious business,

while the singer goes on bringing the news
                              that all the clichés are true

and the sunsets are breaking their old records for beauty.

Two Trains

Then there was that song called "Two Trains Running,"
a Mississippi blues they play on late-night radio,
that program after midnight called *FM in the AM,*
—well, I always thought it was about *trains.*

Then somebody told me it was about what a man and woman do
under the covers of their bed, moving back and forth
like slow pistons in a shiny black locomotive,
the rods and valves trying to stay coordinated

long enough that they will "get to the station"
at the same time. And one of the trains
goes out of sight into the mountain tunnel,
but when they break back into the light

the other train has somehow pulled ahead,
the two trains running like that, side by side,
first one and then the other, with the fierce white
bursts of smoke puffing from their stacks,
into a sky so sharp and blue you want to die.

So then for a long time I thought the song was about sex.

But then Mack told me that all train songs
are really about Jesus, about how the second train
is shadowing the first, so He walks in your footsteps
and He watches you from behind, He is running with you,

He is your brakeman and your engineer,
your coolant and your coal,
and He will catch you when you fall,
and when you stall He will push you through
the darkest mountain valley, up the steepest hill,

and the rough *chuff chuff* of His fingers on the washboard
and the harmonica *woo woo* is the long soul cry by which He
pulls you through the bloody tunnel of the world.
So then I thought the two trains song was a gospel song.

Then I quit my job in Santa Fe and Sharon drove
her spike heel through my heart
and I got twelve years older and Dean moved away,
and now I think the song might be about good-byes—

because we are not even in the same time zone,
or moving at the same speed, or perhaps even
headed toward the same destination—
forgodsakes, we are not even trains!

What grief it is to love some people like your own
blood, and then to see them simply disappear;
to feel time bearing us away
                    one boxcar at a time.

And sometimes, sitting in my chair
I can feel the absence stretching out in all directions—
like the deaf, defoliated silence
just after a train has thundered past the platform,

just before the mindless birds begin to chirp again
—and the wildflowers that grow beside the tracks
wobble wildly on their little stems,
            then gradually grow still and stand

motherless and vertical in the middle of everything.

Rap Music

Twenty-six men trapped in a submarine
are pounding on the walls with a metal pipe,
shouting what they'll do when they get out.
Or they are rolled up in a rug in the back
of a rug truck that has wrecked.

No, it's the car pulled up next to mine in traffic
with the windows rolled down and the sound turned up
so loud it puts everything in italics: enough to make the asphalt thump
and the little leaves of shrubbery
in front of the nice brick houses quake.

I don't know what's going on inside that portable torture chamber,
but I have a bad suspicion
there's a lot of dead white people in there

on a street lit by burning police cars
where a black man is striking the head of a white one
again and again with a brick,
then lifting the skull to drink blood from the hole—

But that's what art is for, isn't it?
It's about giving *expression* to the *indignation*—
it's for taking the *in* out of *inhibitchin*;
so maybe my ears are just a little hysterical
or maybe my fear is a little historical

and you know, I'd like to form an exploratory committee
to investigate that question—
and I'd like that committee to produce a documentary
called *The Sweet Sounds of Afro-America,*

but all this ugly noise is getting in the way,
and what I'm not supposed to say
is that Black for me is a country
more foreign than China or Vagina,
more alarming than going down Niagara on Viagra—

and it makes me feel stupid when I get close
like a little white dog on the edge of a big dark woods
I'm not supposed to look directly into

and there's this pounding noise
like a heartbeat full of steroids,
like a thousand schizophrenic Shakespeares
killing themselves at high volume—

this tangled roar
that has to be shut up or blown away or sealed off
or actually mentioned and entered.

Hate Hotel

Sometimes I like to think about the people I hate.
I take my room at the Hate Hotel, and sit and flip
through the heavy pages of the photographs,
the rogue's gallery of the faces I loathe.

My lamp of resentment sputters twice, then comes on strong,
filling the room with its red light.
That's how hate works—it thrills you and kills you

with its deep heat. Sometimes I like to sit and soak
in the Jacuzzi of my hate, hatching my plots
like a general running his hands over a military map—

and my bombers have been sent out
over the dwellings of my foes,
and are releasing their cargo of ill will

on the targets below, the hate bombs falling in silence
into the lives of the hate-
recipients. From the high window of my office
in the Government of Hate,

where I stay up late, working hard,
where I make no bargains, entertain no
scenarios of reconciliation,

I watch the hot flowers flare up across
the city, the state and continent—
I sip my soft drink of hate on the rocks
and let the punishment go on unstopped,

—again and again I let hate
get pregnant and give birth
to hate, which gets pregnant
and gives birth again—

and only after I feel that hate
has trampled the land, burned it down
to some kingdom come of cautery and ash,
only after it has waxed and waned and waxed all night,

only then can I let hate
creep back in the door. Curl up at my feet
and sleep. Little pussycat hate. Home sweet hate.

Poem in Which I Make the Mistake of Comparing Billie Holiday to a Cosmic Washerwoman

We were driving back from the record store at the mall
when Terrance told me that Billie Holiday
was not a symbol for the black soul.

He said, The night is not African American either, for your information,

it is just goddamn dark,
and in the background

she was singing a song I never heard before,
moving her voice like water moving
along the shore of a lake,
reaching gently into the crevices, touching the pebbles and sand.

Once through the dirty window of a train
on the outskirts of Hoboken, New Jersey,
I swear I saw a sonnet written high up on a concrete wall,

rhymed quatrains rising from the
dyslexic alphabet of gang signs and obscenities,

and Terrance says he saw a fresco
of brown and white angels flying
on a boarded-up building in Chinatown

and everybody knows
there's a teenage genius somewhere out there,
a firebrand out of Ghana by way of Alabama,
this very minute in a warehouse loft,
rewriting *Moby-Dick—The Story of the Great Black Whale*.

When he bursts out of the womb
                              of his American youth
with his dictionary and his hip-hop shovel,

when he takes his place on stage,
dripping the amniotic fluid of history,
he won't be any color we ever saw before,

and I know he's right, Terrance is right, it's so obvious.

But here in the past of that future,
Billie Holiday is still singing
                          a song so dark and slow
it seems bigger than her, it sounds very heavy

like a terrible stain soaked into the sheets,
so deep that nothing will ever get it out,
but she keeps trying,

she keeps pushing the dark syllables under the water
then pulling them up to see if they are clean
but they never are
and it makes her sad
and we are too

and it's dark around the car and inside also is very dark.
Terrance and I can barely see each other
in the dashboard glow.
I can only imagine him right now
pointing at the radio
as if to say, Shut up and listen.

Suicide Song

But now I am afraid I know too much to kill myself
Though I would still like to jump off a high bridge

At midnight, or paddle a kayak out to sea
Until I turn into a speck, or wear a necktie made of knotted rope

But people would squirm, it would hurt them in some way,
And I am too knowledgeable now to hurt people imprecisely.

No longer do I live by the law of me,
No longer having the excuse of youth or craziness,

And dying you know shows a serious ingratitude
For sunsets and beehive hairdos and the precious green corrugated

Pickles they place at the edge of your plate.
Killing yourself is wasteful, like spilling oil

At sea or not recycling all the kisses you've been given,
And anyway, who has clothes nice enough to be caught dead in?

Not me. You stay alive you stupid asshole
Because you haven't been excused,

You haven't finished though it takes a mulish stubbornness
To chew this food.

It is a stone, it is an inconvenience, it is an innocence,
And I turn against it like a record

Turns against the needle
That makes it play.

Fire

The rock band set off fireworks as part of their show—
the ceiling tile of the nightclub smoldered and flared up
over the heads of all those dancing bodies below—

then they churned and burned against the exit doors,
doors someone had chained shut to prevent the would-be sneakers-in—
so 95 party people died that night,

and two days later the weeping girl at the televised funeral
says of her dead friend David,
God must have needed some good rock and roll in heaven.

On earth, God must have needed some good clichés, too,
and weeping riot girls with runny mascara and spiderweb tattoos.
He must have needed the entertainment of dueling insurance companies

calculating the liability per body bag,
and the rock band and nightclub owner pointing fingers at each other
    like guns
and pulling the blame-trigger, *blam blam blam,*

because death is something that always has to be enclosed
by an elaborate set of explanations.
It is an ancient litigation,

this turning of horror into stories,
and it is a lonely piece of work,
trying to turn the stories back into horror,

but somebody has to do it
—especially now that God
has reverted to a state of fire.

Fortune

Like in the Chinese restaurant, it is
the perfect forethought and timing with which
the slices of orange arrive
on a small plate with the bill.

So, while you are paying what is owed,
the sweet juice fills your mouth for free.

And the fortune cookie too
which offers you the pleasure of Breakage
and then the other pleasure of Discovery,

extracting and reading the little strip of paper
with a happiness that you maybe conceal,
the way the child you once were
is even now concealed inside you.

Maybe you will marry a red-haired woman.
Maybe you are going to take a long journey.
Maybe a red-haired woman will steal your car and take a long journey.
Maybe you will be buried next to your mother.

And when the people you are dining with
smile and read their fortunes out loud,
and ask you to tell them your own,
            you smile and tell them a lie,

and they laugh and think you are weird and funny and sad
and you know that you
                        are all of those things,

but you don't tell them the truth
because you don't trust anyone,
                        and you never have:
that is your fortune.

Disappointment

I was feeling pretty religious
standing on the bridge in my winter coat
looking down at the gray water:
the sharp little waves dusted with snow,
fish in their tin armor.

That's what I like about disappointment:
the way it slows you down,
when the querulous insistent chatter of desire
                              goes dead calm

and the minor roadside flowers
pronounce their quiet colors,
and the red dirt of the hillside glows.

She played the flute, he played the fiddle
and the moon came up over the barn.
Then he didn't get the job,—
or her father died before she told him
                that one, most important thing—

and everything got still.

It was February or October
It was July
I remember it so clear
You don't have to pursue anything ever again
It's over
You're free
You're unemployed

You just have to stand there
looking out on the water

in your trench coat of solitude
with your scarf of resignation
                    lifting in the wind.

IV. Luck

The News

The big country beat the little country up
like a schoolyard bully,
so an even bigger country stepped in
and knocked it on its ass to make it nice,
which reminds me of my Uncle Bob's
                              philosophy of parenting.

It's August, I'm sitting on the porch swing,
touching the sores inside my mouth
with the tip of my tongue, watching the sun
go down in the west like a sinking ship,
from which a flood of sticky orange bleeds out.

It's the hour of meatloaf perfume emanating from the houses.
It's the season of Little League practice
and atonal high-school band rehearsals.
You can't buy a beach umbrella in the stores till next year.
The summer beauty pageants are all over,
and no one I know won the swimsuit competition.

This year illness just flirted with me,
picking me up and putting me down
like a cat with a ball of yarn,
so I walked among the living like a tourist,
and I wore my health
like a borrowed shirt,
knowing I would probably have to give it back.

There are the terrible things that happen to you
and the terrible things that you yourself make happen,
like George, who bought a little red sportscar
for his favorite niece
                to smash her life to pieces in.

And the girl on the radio sings,
You know what I'm talking about. Bawhoop, awhoop.

This year it seems like everyone is getting tattoos—
sharks and Chinese characters,
hummingbirds and musical notes—
but the tattoo I would like to get
is of a fist and a rose.

But I can't tell how they will fit together on my shoulder:
if the rose is inside the fist, it will be crushed or hidden;
if the fist is closed,—as a fist by definition is, —
it cannot reach out and touch the rose.

Yet the only tattoo I want
is of a fist and rose, together.
Fist, that helps you survive.
Rose, without which
                  you have no reason to.

Spring Lemonade

In late April they spread manure on the fields
the same week the lilac hedges bloom,
so the nose gets one of those symphonic challenges
that require you to stand out on the porch and breathe.

The earth goes around a corner, the dresser drawers slide out
and naturally, we change our clothes,
putting the long underwear away,
taking out the short-sleeve shirts,

trying to make the transition
from psychological Moscow
                    to psychological Hawaii.

When Mary left her husband in December,
she made herself despise him
as a way of pushing off,
like you would push off from the wall of a swimming pool,

but then she gradually believed her own story
of how horrible he was,

and when I talked to her in March,
she was still spitting on his memory:
you would have thought she never had a heart.

There's a wheel turning in the center of the earth
and over it, our feet are always running, running,
trying to keep pace.
Then there's a period of quietude and rue,
when you want to crawl inside yourself,
when you prefer ugliness to hope.

Last night the sunset was so pink and swollen
the sky looked like it had gotten an infection.

We were sitting on the lawn and sipping lemonade.
Inflamed clouds were throbbing in the fevered light.
Shannon murmured, *Somebody better call a doctor.*
Kath said, *Someody get some aspirin.*
But nobody moved.

And the smell of lilacs and manure blew out of the fields
with such complexity and sweetness, we closed our eyes.
It had nothing to do with being good, or smart, or choosing right.
It had to do with being lucky—
something none of us had ever imagined.

Catechism for November

In the movie theater one night, you whispered,
        "It is easier to watch than to live,"
and on the street outside, you thought,
        "If this was a book, I would skip this part."

Remember when you opened the fortune cookie in March?
      It said, "Ideology is bad for you."
Remember when you called Anabelle
      "an encyclopedia of self-perpetuating pain?"

On Tuesday you said, "I'm a small wooden boat,
      adrift in the space between storms,"
and on Wednesday you said, "I should go to the park more often."

Then you killed the spider with the heel of your shoe,
and said, "I can't take care of all sentient beings!"

But when the girl with pink hair brought her sniffles to class,
you found a Kleenex in your purse for her.

This is how it happens: one at a time,
the minutes come out of the box where they were hidden:
      the witty ones with yellow feathers;
            the thick gray ones with no horizon.

But once you swore, "I want to see it all, unsentimentally."
Once you wrote in your green notebook,
      "Let me start in the middle, again."

Narcissus Lullaby

If someone anywhere right now
is imagining me,
saying my name thoughtfully,

with her pink tongue touching
the smooth ceiling of her mouth
softly to pronounce the *T,*

like the first brush stroke
in a figurative landscape painting of
He-Who-Is-the-Subject-of-This-Poem,

—then I can relax a moment
in the matter of remembering myself,
I can close my eyes and let

the whole factory of identity go
drifting in the dark
like a big brick warehouse full of anxious secrets

in an unsafe neighborhood
gone quiet at the end of day,
yet guarded and protected and caressed

by the softly conscious flashlight
of my imaginary friend's
imagination.

Windchime

She goes out to hang the windchime
in her nightie and her work boots.
It's six-thirty in the morning
and she's standing on the plastic ice chest
tiptoe to reach the crossbeam of the porch,

windchime in her left hand,
hammer in her right, the nail
gripped tight between her teeth
but nothing happens next because
she's trying to figure out
how to switch #1 with #3.

She must have been standing in the kitchen,
coffee in her hand, asleep,
when she heard it—the wind blowing
through the sound the windchime
wasn't making
because it wasn't there.

No one, including me, especially anymore believes
till death do us part,
but I can see what I would miss in leaving—
the way her ankles go into the work boots
as she stands upon the ice chest;
the problem scrunched into her forehead;
the little kissable mouth
with the nail in it.

Physiology of Kisses

The kiss begins   in the center of the belly
and travels upwards   through the diaphragm and throat
along fine filaments   which no forensic scientist
has ever been able to find.

From the hard flower   of the kisser's mouth,
the kisses leave the body   in single file,
into the reciprocal mouth   of the kiss-recipient,
which for me is Kath.

What can I say? My kisses make her happy and I need that.
And sometimes, bending over her,
I have the unmistakable impression
                  that I am watering a plant,

gripping myself softly   by the handle,
tilting my spout   forward
pouring what I need to give
            into the changing shape of her thirst.

I keep leaning forward   to pour out
what continues to rise up
from the fountain   of the kisses
which I, also,   am drinking from.

How It Adds Up

There was the day we swam in a river, a lake, and an ocean.
And the day I quit the job my father got me.
And the day I stood outside a door,
and listened to my girlfriend making love
to someone obviously not me, inside,

and I felt strange because I didn't care.

There was the morning I was born,
and the year I was a loser,
and the night I was the winner of the prize
for which the audience applauded.

Then there was someone else I met,
whose face and voice I can't forget,
and the memory of her
is like a jail I'm trapped inside,

or maybe she is something I just use
                    to hold my real life at a distance.

Happiness, Joe says, *is a wild red flower*
            plucked from a river of lava
and held aloft on a tightrope
            strung between two scrawny trees
above a canyon
            in a manic-depressive windstorm.

Don't drop it, Don't drop it, Don't drop it—,

And when you do, you will keep looking for it
everywhere, for years,
while right behind you,
the footprints you are leaving

will look like notes
                    of a crazy song.

Man Carrying Sofa

Whatever happened to Cindy Morrison, that nice young lesbian?
I heard she moved to the city and got serious.
Traded in her work boots for high heels and a power suit.
Got a health-care plan and an attorney girlfriend.

Myself, I don't want to change.
It's January and I'm still dating my checks November.
I don't want to step through the doorway of the year.
I'm afraid of something falling off behind me.
I'm afraid my own past will start forgetting me.

Now the sunsets are like cranberry sauce
poured over the yellow hills, and yes,
that beauty is so strong it hurts—
it hurts because it isn't personal.

But we look anyway, we sit upon our stoops
and stare, —fierce,
like we were tossing down a shot of vodka, straight,
and afterwards, we feel purified and sad and rather Russian.

When David was in town last week,
I made a big show to him of how unhappy I was
because I wanted him to go back and tell Susan
that I was suffering without her—

but then he left and I discovered
I really was miserable
—which made me feel better about myself—
because, after all, I don't want to go through time untouched.

What a great journey this is,
this ordinary life of ants and sandwich wrappers,
of X-rated sunsets and drive-through funerals.

And this particular complex pain inside your chest;
this damaged longing
like a heavy piece of furniture inside you;
you carry it, it burdens you, it drags you down—
then you stop, and rest on top of it.

Grammar of Sparrows

The sparrows are a kind of people
Who lost a war a thousand years ago;
As punishment all their color was taken away;

Brown and beige and gray they cling now to the slender
Stalks of cattails in the marsh, hard to see
Against the shifting tawny grass.

I have to drive two hours to the shore,
Past the naked trampled-looking fields of stubble corn,
The run-down failing farms,
The water in the ditches standing still and full

Under a sky the eighteen colors of October,
All of them gray—

When Em said, "My plans were changed for me,"
And looked down at her hands; when Bethany said,
"He loves me in the wrong way,"
It was this kind of day inside of us: off-season:

House for Rent, Unfurnished;
Leaning single mailbox driveway;
Lakeside cafe Closed for Personal Reasons.

And the birds like little defeated soldiers
                    hiding in the chest-high weeds.

When the sparrows rise up for no apparent reason
And circle small and high against the pale vast sky,
What makes it so important?

As if my sadness was an endangered species;
As if my mood was a coastal wetlands area
in need of federal protection;

A place never intended for development,
Meant always to be useless.

This is what I left behind when I went forward.
When I feel good for nothing now,
I come back here to stand and look at it:

Wet and still like a footprint in the mud;
Hard to see inside the moving browns;
Lying low like an understanding.

The Time Wars

It was the winter we ate a lot of oatmeal to stay warm.
We lived on 17th and G Streets; Kath called it the G spot.
At night in the bathtub I read *The Collected Letters of Virginia Woolf*,
trying to keep the pages of 20th-century prose from getting wet,
reading the guest lists for her dinner parties
as she knocked out book after book between her shattering depressions.

Sometimes I would meet Richard at the Chinese place for dinner,
and one two three hours would vanish like our food.
We would stand outside The Great Wall, adjusting our scarves
in a pastoral moment of urban separation,
watching the cabs whiz by in the dusk.

The Vietnam War monument was just five blocks away;
on Saturday you would always see a vet or two,
in their windbreakers and baseball caps—
heads down, crying in the shrubs—
the little POW buttons and various insignia attached to their clothing
like they were advertising something.

We ourselves were fighting the Time Wars:
we could feel it speeding up, rapidly escaping,
like the hiss from a leaky balloon.
We were trying to plug it, to slow it down, to decelerate,
but none of us was having much success—

One day in February Kath brought in some roses and said,
"Here, the sun came 93 million miles
to make these flowers that I killed for you,"
and I said, "Kathleen, my talents are not capacious enough
to properly exaggerate your virtues,"
and we both burst out laughing
and time stopped right over our heads like a little red car.

On June 14th, 1940, Virginia Woolf wrote in her journal,
"Windy day. I am the hare, far ahead of my critics, the hounds."
Something endearing about the mixture of weather report and vanity.
Something lonely about this image of success.

We ourselves aren't thinking about the future anymore.
What we want is to calm time down, to get time in a good mood,
to make time feel wanted.
We just want to give time many homemade gifts,
covered with fingerprints and kisses.

TONY HOAGLAND is the author of two other books of poems, *Sweet Ruin* (1992) and *Donkey Gospel* (1998), which received the James Laughlin Award of The Academy of American Poets. He has recently joined the faculty of the University of Houston, and he has taught for many years in the Warren Wilson College low-residency M.F.A. program. A book of prose about poetry, *Real Sofistikashun*, is near completion.

The text of these poems has been set in Janson, a typeface designed by Miklós Kis, a major figure in typography in Holland as well as in his native Hungary. He spent most of the 1680s in Amsterdam where he learned the craft.

Book design by Wendy Holdman
Composition by BookMobile Design and Publishing Services,
Minneapolis, Minnesota
Manufacturing by Thomson-Shore on acid-free paper